Minute Motivators for Leaders

Stan Toler

BEACON HILL PRESS
OF KANSAS CITY

Copyright © 2002, 2011, 2014 by Stan Toler

Beacon Hill Press of Kansas City
PO Box 419527
Kansas City, MO 64141
www.BeaconHillBooks.com

ISBN 978-0-8341-3284-9

Printed in the
United States of America

Library of Congress Control Number: 2014941401

The Internet addresses, email addresses, and phone numbers in this book are accurate at the time of publication. They are provided as a resource. Beacon Hill Press of Kansas City does not endorse them or vouch for their content or permanence.

10 9 8 7 6 5 4 3 2 1

Introduction

Leaders don't have all the answers, though others may think they do.

Leadership isn't about showing people how energetic, enthusiastic, or entrepreneurial you are. It's about gaining enough knowledge and wisdom to move people and plans from obscurity to excellence. Leaders are always on the learning curve. They know they haven't arrived until they've shown someone else by their own example how to be the best they can be.

Minute Motivators for Leaders is a friend for the journey. It offers proven and progressive principles for finding your way through the uncertainty of the times.

Stan Toler

Leaders rub shoulders with great leaders.

"Anyone who influences others is a leader."

—Chuck Swindoll

ASSOCIATION

If we are known by the company we keep, then the company we keep ought to inspire and invigorate us to greatness. Leadership is not just learned by scanning words, sentences, or paragraphs in a textbook. It is grasped by the mind and spirit of those who search for it in the lives of others. Aspiring leaders recognize the importance of keeping company with those who have chosen to excel. They listen to them, watch them. They seek them out. Their words and actions fall on their spirits like drops of moisture on a thirsty sponge.

Aspiring leaders acknowledge that the achievement of others offers a key to unlocking their own excellence. They associate with great men and women not as an act of worship but rather to learn the cause of their success. Every leader should be a mentor. But more important, every leader should *have* a mentor.

Call it success by association—the people who strive for personal excellence will find a way to rub shoulders with the great people around them.

Leaders do the right things.

"Reputation is made in
a moment. Character is
built in a lifetime."

—James Leggett

CHARACTER

Lots of people can get the job done. Industry, science, education—each profession has its stellar achievers. Personal competence is not a rare quality these days. Newspapers and professional journals chronicle the personal best of these dedicated men and women. But personal *character* is becoming rather elusive. Like the biblical Esau, some professionals have traded the inheritance of their reputations for the pottage of dollars and cents. They've become day traders, bartering the wealth of the eternal for the pittance of the temporary.

"If it's worth doing, it's worth doing right," the ancient leadership adage demands. But leaders of character are more concerned with *doing the right* thing than they are in *doing things right*. Right methods without right motives are shallow at best and evil at their worst. In the end, the great leader is not the person who can simply get the job done. It is the person who knows how to link motives with methods.

Leadership that makes a difference includes a personal willingness to do the right thing. It makes tough choices—moral choices, spiritual choices, ethical choices, right choices.

Leaders make everyone feel valuable.

"A great man shows his greatness by the way he treats little men."

—Thomas Carlyle

AFFIRMATION

Leaders understand that every member of their team has an innate need to be valued, recognized, included. Each team member is a star in the leader's eyes. Consequently, everyone on the team is treated with the respect afforded a volunteer, no matter what their pay scale is. Leaders are the first to recognize the achievement of others. They are lavish with handshakes and smiles, diligent with dialogue and encouragement, noteworthy in their note writing. They understand that a "spoonful of sugar" makes even the mundane and tasteless tasks of their subordinates more tolerable.

Leaders also understand the importance of a name. They realize that personal *attention* begins with a personal *salutation*. To them, coworkers are not anonymous entities, valued only for their contribution. They are valued friends. True leadership seeks to affirm the individual worth of colleagues and associates. It lets them know that they truly belong—that they are more than nine-to-five residents in some netherworld of carpeted cubicles.

Effective leaders have come to realize that a pat on the back has enough force to propel an associate toward excellence.

Leaders know what to do next.

"Leadership is calculated
risk-taking."

—Ted Ward

FORESIGHT

A chess master never thinks only of the next move. He is thinking three, four, or five moves ahead. Leaders do the same thing. Their vision is cast well into the future. And that future is as familiar to them as it can be to the finite mind. They have dreamed dreams of that place. They have planted and built their hopes there. They have already envisioned a completion in that future.

Leaders aren't that enthused about short trips. They are on a long journey of excellence. And they know that journey is made of individual steps, each firmly planted in uncharted territory.

In one sense, they never arrive. When one phase of a project is completed, they instantly move to the next. When a goal is achieved, they roll out the new one. No problem is ever the end of the road. No achievement is ever the top of the hill. There is always that next step— the step already dreamed in their heart; the step planned for, prayed for, and provided for, because of the far-reaching vision.

Leaders grow leaders.

"You've got to have great athletes to win, I don't care who the coach is. You can't win without good athletes, but you can lose with them. This is where coaching makes the difference."

—Lou Holtz

MENTORING

You can always spot an A-level leader. How? He or she will have A-level subordinates. Those who follow them will have some of their skills, some of their determination, and some of their vision. True leadership is contagious. People catch it, and it germinates in their spirits.

You can spot B-level leaders just as easily. They'll probably have C-level subordinates. B-level leaders are intimidated by the potential of others. They are micromanagers, keepers of the keys who prevent the unlocking of someone's potential. Their own insecurity covers over the blossoming of visionaries like a heavy woolen blanket.

A-level leaders are not threatened by great potential. In fact, they look for it, seek it, recruit it, and develop it. It thrills them. It drives them on to even greater accomplishments. They have discovered the secret of excellence. They have realized the great possibility—that they can multiply their work by developing and training their associates to reach their full capability.

A great leader will not be a leader of followers. He or she will be a leader of leaders.

Leaders network with other leaders.

"I not only use all the brains
that I have, but all that
I can borrow."

—Woodrow Wilson

NETWORKING

Leaders know the facts of life: First, most of the productivity comes from a cadre of effective people; second, most of the decisions in an organization are made by a handful of respected leaders; third, the pipeline to achievement is learning to recognize those circles of influence and seeking to penetrate them.

The process is important. Aspiring leaders make it a point to identify the leaders in an organization. Who is making a mark on the corporation? Whose ideas generate the interest of others? Whom do the associates gravitate toward? Once that circle of influence is identified, the aspiring leader seeks to form a spiritual network.

They work with the circle members, investing time and effort in helping them reach their goals. They share information with them, insights that eventually will be reciprocated. And most important, they learn from them. They copy their best, and they sort out their worst through filters of character and spiritual commitments.

Networking—great leaders have learned the truth in the old maxim, "It's not only *what* you know, but *who* you know that counts."

Leaders are visionary.

"Anyone can steer the ship,
but it takes a real leader
to chart the course."

—George Barna

VISION

Leaders not only have an eye on the horizon, they can see just beyond it. Their firm grasp of the present is based on their never-ending hope for the future. They can deal with things as they are because they have dreamed of what they can be.

They have a vision. "Without it," the scriptures say, "people perish." One of the marks of leadership is the ability to look beyond the immediate to a better, brighter tomorrow. For example, leaders look at vacant land and see a thriving business. They see a skeletal framework and envision a skyscraper. They meet with a casual acquaintance and anticipate a future partnership.

Leaders are not satisfied with the status quo. They have an inner desire for the next level. Time and inconvenience are mere pawns to be moved toward the ultimate capture. Leaders imagine a future that is better than the present—and they look for ways to make it happen.

Leaders are not that interested in what's happening *now*. They're more interested in what's happening *next*.

Leaders are willing to take a risk.

"Life without risks is
not worth living."

—Charles A. Lindbergh

VENTURE

"If you don't want to run with the big dogs, then stay on the porch." Whoever coined that saying understood this tenet of leadership: It's risky.

The paths of opportunity have a few speed bumps. Plans fail. Funding evaporates. Markets change. Allies desert. It's a jungle out there! But great leaders have learned to be survivalists. They nourish themselves as they can. They form alliances. They envision a strategy. They resist surrender.

Leaders understand the risk and are willing to take it. They know that life doesn't come with a money-back guarantee, that there is no guarantee of success in any endeavor. But they're still willing to lead the charge. They're willing to convince people that battles can be won in spite of the size or the armament of the enemy.

Leaders are willing to pay a price. They're prepared to barter what they have for what they might gain. They're motivated more by the prospect of success than by the fear of failure. They're adventurers. They're not willing to stay on the porch.

Leaders are inspirational in style.

"Motivation is like the tide.
It raises everyone up when
it comes in."

—Bill Burch

MOTIVATION

There are three ways to motivate people: guilt, flattery, and inspiration. Most of us have been booked on one or more guilt trips. And from experience, we know that the journey wasn't all that pleasant. "But we really need you." "Everyone else is helping." "You really owe it to us." Cooperation by coercion is not true cooperation. It may prompt a desired action, but it certainly does not prompt a desired result.

Even flattery can be a negative motivator. "You'll get a lot of recognition for this." "Everyone says you do this so well." "All the credit will go to you." These comments are praise placebos, one-handed applause. Leaders know how important it is to reinforce the team effort with honest recognition, but they don't hand out bouquets of plastic roses.

Great leaders inspire their followers. "I have a dream!" "Think of what we can accomplish!" "You can contribute to something great!"

Either by word or by deed, the best leaders are those who can inspire others to reach for something greater than themselves.

Leaders
forgive quickly.

"He who cannot forgive breaks
the bridge over which he
himself must pass."

—Tom Eliff

CHARITY

Little people carry grudges. Great people forgive and forget. Little people hold on to insults. Great people let them go. Little people nurture thoughts of revenge. Great people move on. Leaders are big people. They're tolerant, indulgent, forgiving. Leaders are charitable.

Sticks and stones break bones; but the fact is, names hurt too. Leaders may not have to dodge the branches or granite thrown by their opposition, but often they can't avoid their hurled insults. The way a leader reacts means the difference between leadership greatness and mediocrity. Reacting with revenge is self-defeating. It only enhances the conflict and leaves the defender with inner turmoil—and fewer friends. Reacting with charity is influential.

Great leaders refuse to don battle gear. Instead, they stay focused on their goal. Great leaders refuse to allow personal insults to distract them. They've abandoned themselves in pursuit of a greater good—the enrichment and welfare of others.

Ask any leader why he or she is willing to forgive and forget, and you'll hear, "I don't have time to be bitter. I only have time to be better."

Leaders are good communicators.

"To be effective, leaders must know how to communicate their visions effectively and how to enlist the cooperation of others."

—M. Z. Hackman and C. E. Johnson

COMMUNICATION

There's no point in having a good idea if you can't tell anybody what it is. Like giving a gift, leaders learn how to take a thought, wrap it in words, and present it to one or more of their associates.

This "communication gift-giving" is both delicate and deliberate. First, the thought must be relevant. It must speak to the issues of the listener. Second, it must be well-wrapped. Leaders learn the language. They are as comfortable with a comma as they are with a question mark. Nouns and verbs are parked in their reserved spaces, and adjectives and adverbs don't embarrass their subjects. Third, the presentation should be clear, concise, correct, and generously decorated with humorous or poignant illustrations.

Good communicators leave no doubt about the meaning of their message. They know that the communication process isn't complete until the audience has both listened and understood the delivered message.

When great leaders communicate, everyone around them knows what's going on. They know because the leader has made sure of it!

Leaders understand people.

"One of the marks of true
greatness is the ability to
develop greatness in others."

—J. C. McCauley

INSIGHT

Leaders are in the people business. Their primary function is not to buy, sell, analyze, minister, or ply a trade. It is to understand and work with people. They know that the road to success is lined with people—people with differing attitudes, abilities, or acumen. The greatest principles or plans on earth are dormant without the cooperative effort of people who are concerned with the blossoming.

A leader asks insightful questions. Why do some whistle, while others whine? Why do some act as seasoning, while others are just salty? Why are some easily moved, while others are immobile?

They observe people. They study their motives, talk with them, and listen to them. They seek to understand what makes them happy, sad, angry, or annoyed.

Leaders know they aren't just hiring or appointing a person. They are inheriting a past, a pain, or a peculiarity. So they look with insight beyond the smiles or frowns—all the way to the heart.

An effective leader can read people the way others read a newspaper.

Leaders are enthusiastic about the future.

"Great leaders are never satisfied with current levels of performance. They are relentlessly driven by possibilities and potential achievements."

—Donna Harrison

EXPECTATION

I've been to the mountaintop, and I've seen the other side." Those words of Dr. Martin Luther King Jr. ignited the passion of the civil rights movement. His attitude of expectancy caused thousands to follow him, no matter what the cost.

What was there about his leadership that made such an impression on his followers? First, he had a positive view of the future. He believed that his dream of equality and justice would one day be realized.

Second, he believed that right would win out. Even as the fires of hatred and oppression burned, King believed that an ultimate good would arise from their ashes.

Third, he believed that his message would be accepted. In spite of immediate rejection, Martin Luther King Jr. envisioned a day when his missive of peace and harmony would be preached, taught, and practiced. He simply expected it to happen.

The task of a leader is to show people the future. Visionary leaders have been to the mountaintop. They have seen the other side, and they can't wait to take others there.

Leaders accentuate the positive.

"Enthusiasm is contagious.
It's difficult to remain neutral
or indifferent in the presence
of a positive thinker."

—Melvin Maxwell

OPTIMISM

The leader always sees the day as sunny, never partly cloudy. Why? Because leaders know optimism is highly contagious. Even in small doses, an attitude that believes for the best can spread quickly and influence many. Pessimists may gather their followers, but they will stay close to home. They're afraid of new roads and far horizons. They feed off their own negative energy, and soon they grow weak and tired.

The optimistic leader, on the other hand, thrives in the pessimist's backyard. He or she knows that a better day is coming. The optimist emits a positive energy flow that is infused into the weary until they become strong.

The team takes its cue from the leader. So, if the leader is negative, the team will be negative too. But if the leader dwells on what's right, the team will share the same positive viewpoint.

There will always be critics to point out what's wrong. It's the leader's job to see what's right.

Leaders are learners.

"If you stop learning today,
you stop leading tomorrow."

—Howard Hendricks

LEARNING

A leader's education never ends with the graduation ceremony. It lasts throughout his or her life. Good leaders are always looking for ways to fill in the gaps in their understanding. They are constantly learning on two different levels: knowledge and skill.

Leaders have a never-quenched thirst for knowledge. They read and ask questions. They study problems, watch others, and think. A leader understands that the mind is the most effective leadership tool, and he sharpens it constantly.

Also, leaders are constantly in training. As skillful as they may be, they constantly tone and train. They seek a racer's edge in their field of endeavor. They practice with the discipline of an athlete. They read the manuals and do the roadwork. They seek the counsel of good coaches—coaches with keen insight who will look for the little, unnoticed flaws and will provide instruction to hone their skills without discouraging them.

Who you know really is important. But *what* you know is the link that ties you to the person.

Leaders seek the collective wisdom of the team.

"Anger and haste hinder
good counsel."

—English Proverb

COUNSEL

If it's true that the lawyer who represents himself has a fool for a client, it is equally true that the leader who advises himself has a fool for a counselor. The Scriptures teach us that there is wisdom in *many* counselors. Each of us has a "web of wisdom" that we may resource for the solution to a problem or the direction of a plan. The web consists of wise and learned relatives, friends, or associates who have graduated from the school of experience.

Nobody succeeds alone. Even the lonely marathon runner has a coach. There are times of concentrated running and times of intense listening. The runner's counsel directly affects his reaching the goal.

The best leaders surround themselves with bright lights. They know that they are not above the advice of their subordinates. Since their team members were chosen because of their knowledge and skill, they are a well of ideas. Good leaders will draw confidently from that well with quiet regularity.

Good leaders know they need advice, and they seek it.

Leaders share success with the team.

"Alone we can do so little;
together we can do so much."

—Helen Keller

PARTNERSHIP

Why do some leaders succeed where others fail? Because they understand that success is a team effort. Leadership and teamwork go hand in glove. One is fully dependent upon the other. Leaders have learned the valued principle of partnership, and they are always ready to team with someone who can contribute to a shared goal.

"Two heads are better than one" is one of the axioms learned early in life. What then is the next level? Four heads? Eight? Sixteen? The pooling of increased wisdom and ability affords a greater opportunity for excellence. Efficiency generally increases with participation.

And when the team leader is credited for that efficiency, true leadership always accepts the accolades on behalf of others. Great leaders understand that sharing the blessing is equally as important as sharing the blame. Praising the team for their efforts simply motivates them to greater efficiency.

Great leaders create an atmosphere in which others can succeed also. They're not afraid to allow their associates to take responsibility, and they're willing to give credit when they excel.

When success comes, leaders celebrate a *team* victory!

Leaders accept pain and disappointment in stride.

"Some people succeed because they are destined to, but most people succeed because they are determined."

—Elmer Towns

ENDURANCE

The best leaders know that they won't always get their own way. Plans will crumble. People will stumble. Sometimes the breaks will go the other way. That's life, and a wise leader learns to accept it and go on. They understand that the victor's crown is given only to those who endure to the end. Endurance is a quality that causes some to make bright new discoveries in the wake of a disaster. For example, in the hands of the scientist, one person's trauma gives birth to technological advancements that give hope to many.

Let's face it, sometimes the walls come tumbling down. What happens next? Attitude will make the difference. Good leaders may become angry, but never irate. They may be discouraged and distracted, but they determine not to be wrathful due to their pain or disappointment. They dig in, regroup, and focus on solutions. They come to grips with their adversity instead of succumbing to it. They keep on keeping on.

Leaders understand that a level head comes from a strong heart.

Leaders create atmosphere.

"A leader is an individual who has an inspiring vision and can get others to buy into it."

—Laurence Smith

MAGNETISM

Leaders don't depend on the weather. They bring the sunshine with them. Truly effective leaders can make their presence felt in any situation. They walk into a room with a determined gait. They look for that first set of eyes with which they can connect. They use a smile to brighten the darkened corners. Their words evoke confidence and encouragement.

Leaders have discovered that they can move people with the power of their presence. They know that when they speak enthusiastically of the future, people will have hope. When they talk of the possibility of success, people will have confidence. When they underscore the positive qualities of an idea, people are motivated.

Leaders understand that magnetism is one part inherited and two parts developed. They live in an atmosphere that is, to some extent, of their own creation. They have learned that by carrying a gray cloud on a string everywhere they go, the people they encounter will naturally be disheartened. But by letting the sun shine through their demeanor, they can cast a confident aura.

Magnetic personalities cause a positive energy flow.

Leaders acknowledge the potential of others.

"Treat people as if they were what they ought to be, and you may help them to become what they are capable of being."

—Johann Wolfgang von Goethe

ENCOURAGEMENT

Humans are the vast untapped resource of the planet. Wise leaders are those who mine that potential. They see what's good in others and bring it to the surface. In many ways, human potential exceeds that of time's great inventions. Leaders see the potential of their associates. They are always more concerned with what someone *will be* than with what he or she currently is.

Leaders see the unmined skills of others as later abilities. As a potter holds the unformed clay and envisions its later excellence, a leader sees his or her associates' weaknesses as future strengths and their questions as future wisdom.

The leader's associates are rough diamonds whose luster needs the polishing of a skilled craftsman. The leader's task is to bring about that polishing. In the process, he or she makes self-fulfilling prophecies which encourage people in ways such as these: "I think you could do this, if you tried." "You'll be our top performer before the year is out." "I believe in you."

Leaders realize that by adding a cup of encouragement, they may reap gallons of achievement.

Leaders take time for recreation and fun.

"A little nonsense now and then
is relished by the wisest men."

—Willy Wonka

RELAXATION

Good leaders don't make slaves of others, and they don't make slaves of themselves. They know that relaxation is not a luxury, it's a necessity. Too much focus and too little time for renewal create a dangerous leadership imbalance. Just as the body needs rest to revitalize its energy, the leader and his or her team need a pause for refreshment.

Good leaders watch over the needs of their team. They make wise suggestions about the team's physical, mental, and spiritual rebuilding times. They evaluate and protect the team's personal, social, and professional balance. They purposefully schedule activities to avoid overexertion and stress.

In the same way, wise leaders take time for themselves. They know the good of a round of golf, the serenity of a set of tennis, the balm of a day at the beach, or the blessing of a good book. These are not perks for the privileged; they are emotional and spiritual tools for self-maintenance.

Relaxation is a good remedy for taking life too seriously. A leader needs a timely "time out."

Leaders solve problems others fear.

"Those who try to do something
and fail are infinitely better
than those who try to do
nothing and succeed."

—Lloyd Jones

CHALLENGE

Leaders love challenges. While others may see challenges as stumbling blocks, leaders see them as stepping-stones. To them, problems are unformed opportunities to create, to re-invent, and to excel. The juices of the leader really start to flow when an obstacle suddenly appears. Like the football lineman who gets an adrenaline rush when the opposing player charges toward him, leaders are instantly motivated to stand against the problems they face.

Leaders see the opposition of an enemy as an opportunity to win a friend. They view the overwhelming elements of a problem as an opportunity to marshal forces against it. Leaders are proactive. They know that the greater the challenge, the greater the sense of accomplishment when it's met.

"Impossible" and "undoable" are words that are not usually on the lips of a true leader. They have a different language. "Yes." "I know we can." "Let's try." Great leaders may be afraid at times, but they never allow their fears to keep them from facing a challenge with courage.

When others are throwing in the towel, the leader is going back to the drawing board.

Leaders are supportive.

"People cannot be managed.
Inventories can be managed,
but people must be led."

—H. Ross Perot

SUPPORT

A good leader has a support system—not just a support system that tends to their personal concerns, but one that looks out for the interests of others. Leaders understand the importance of taking someone with them as they climb the ladder of success.

They not only delight in the success of others; they actually create an environment that fosters it. Leaders are tireless motivators. As the farmer diligently tends the crop, so the leader cultivates the team. Time and convenience are easily sacrificed for the cause of developing a champion.

Leaders are quick to offer praise, personal advice, and words of support. They know the value of a positive note, e-mail, or telephone call. They understand one of the basic motivators: recognition. They're quick to say, "Thank you." "I appreciate you" flows naturally from their lips. They make their associates feel vital to the cause.

Unsuccessful leaders resort to blame, anger, and criticism in order to control people. Successful leaders set people free by supporting them.

Leaders have a sense of humor.

"Humor is to life what shock absorbers are to automobiles."

—Stan Toler

HUMOR

Good leaders don't take themselves too seriously. They know how to laugh and are willing to laugh at themselves. Since they have a firm grip on who they are and what they are about, they aren't threatened by the understanding that their associates are keenly aware of their foibles and probably have had a laugh or two at their expense.

Good leaders know that a bit of measured silliness can break the bondage of prolonged seriousness. A carefully chosen, well-placed joke or humorous story can instantly reverse the negative mood of a meeting. Humor is also effective in breaking down the walls between leadership and the team. A shared joke with the team may not only calm a tense situation, it can create rapport and cultivate trust. When the leader laughs, the team shares a sense of relief.

Nobody trusts a leader who doesn't know how to laugh. Lincoln had a sharp wit. Kennedy kidded with the press. The greatest leaders are content with themselves and are able to smile.

Leaders model leadership.

"I'd rather see a sermon than hear one any day."

—David O. McKay

EXAMPLE

Some of the greatest lessons in leadership are seen and not heard. The classroom of daily life is one of the most ideal settings for learning about directing others toward their goals. Lessons learned there have the edge of being more practical and fundamental than those found in a textbook alone. Actual work or ministry situations are the greatest of all illustrations.

Good leaders don't just preach about excellence; they practice it. The qualities they desire in their associates are qualities that they have modeled in their own lives. They have a good work ethic. They're punctual and diligent. They keep their word and finish the job they've started. They're efficient.

Good leaders enjoy the respect of the team by demonstrating excellence in all aspects of life. Because they are human, leaders will let others down at times. But because they have leadership qualities, they will seek to keep their personal standards high enough for their associates to look up to.

Leaders share knowledge and experience by their actions as well as their words.

Leaders aim for excellence.

"Whatever is worth doing
at all is worth doing well."

—Philip Chesterfield

EXCELLENCE

Leaders are never willing to settle for second best. They always believe that something worth doing is worth doing well. They start a task thoughtfully, continue it diligently, and finish it thoroughly. Each step from the inception to the benediction is a commitment to excellence.

Leaders know that excellence is learned. Just as the scientist trains his or her mind to understand theories and methods to accomplish some scientific achievement, leaders commit themselves to the theories and methods necessary to reach their organization's goal. They train themselves to focus on the plans and techniques for accomplishing their purpose. They make personal sacrifices for corporate success.

Leaders also understand that excellence is a quality rather than a quantity. It's a state of mind. It reaches as far as it can and accomplishes as much as possible. Leaders know they run the risk of not reaching the expectations of their peers, but they rest in knowing they have done their very best.

Leaders aren't content to go for the silver. They like the feel of real gold.

Leaders love to celebrate.

"Celebrate the happiness that friends are always giving, make every day a holiday and celebrate just living."

—Amanda Bradley

CELEBRATION

A leader will pick just about any reason to throw a party. He or she knows that nothing builds morale like a celebration, no matter how small. Whether it's a box of bagels, a picnic in the park, or a surprise afternoon off, leaders understand the motivating force of publicly acknowledging a job well done.

Leaders celebrate a good performance by the team, the completion of a goal, or even the completion of one objective. They take delight in honoring the corporate achievements of those who have worked together in achieving a common goal. There are many ways to say, "Great work, team!" And good leaders will use as many of those ways as possible.

Leaders delight in honoring individual achievements as well. They recognize the hard work of an individual by a public and tangible commemoration of the effort.

Leaders love personal celebrations too. They affirm people at every opportunity by celebrating birthdays, extracurricular achievements, or family milestones. They write, call, or send a gift.

Leaders have a heart for honoring others.

Leaders lead people, not institutions.

"True leadership must be for the benefit of the people, not the enrichment of the institution."

—Loren Gresham

MOVEMENT

Bureaucrats run institutions. Leaders lead people. There's a great difference. Bureaucrats shuffle and tab papers with a sense of glee. Their computer hard drives are crammed with memorandums and tickler files. They move through the forests of white boards and easels like gazelles. Sadly, they are captives of their own corporations. The institution is a cold entity. It takes instead of gives. It's self-preserving and focused on the bottom line.

Leaders would rather work with people than paper. People are dynamic. They have the capacity to give as well as receive. People need to be led. They are incomplete without direction.

Institutions stifle leadership. Real leaders are dreamers, risk takers. They want to see movement. Reports, committees, departments —leaders see these things as necessary evils. But their real passion is for people. They delight in helping their coworkers reach their destinations. They are fueled by the smiles of accomplishment. They joy in the "yes!" moments with their associates.

A real leader longs not for an organization to run, but for a people to lead.

Leaders are listeners.

"The first step to wisdom is silence; the second is listening."

—Carl Summer

ATTENTIVENESS

Here's a quick test of leadership. Does the leader look into the eyes of the person speaking to him or her? If so, the leader is attentive, interested, and concerned about the needs of the team member. If not, the leader is distracted, unconcerned, or egotistical. Good leaders take people seriously. They listen carefully to the words, inflection, and emotions expressed by others.

Leaders listen to the ideas of their associates. They may not act on every suggestion they receive, but they listen with an ear to hear fresh methodologies. They understand that a concept that may propel them upwards may very well come from a member of their team.

They also listen to complaints. Leaders understand that emotions left unvented can be explosive and stifling or could very well suffocate the efforts of the rest of the team. They value the feedback of both team members and critics. They understand that the cries and concerns of others are cries for personal attention.

Leaders learn because they listen.

Leaders are observers.

"A leader is the one who
climbs the tallest tree,
surveys the entire situation,
and yells, 'wrong jungle!'"

—Stephen Covey

ALERTNESS

What is the leader doing while the team is hard at work? Watching. But don't confuse watching people work with doing nothing. Good leaders are keen observers —they're alert.

First, they watch the workers. They are alert to see who produces and who doesn't. They watch for weakness in order to strengthen, and they watch for strengths in order to capitalize on them.

Second, they study the process. They want to see what works and what doesn't. They are alert to tired methods and outdated machinery. They value the introduction of new routines for accomplishing established tasks. They know fresh production methods will result in new products.

Third, they are alert to the upcoming leadership in the organization. They notice those who have a passion to excel. Leaders know that by observing the interaction of skills and personalities, outstanding personalities will evolve with the potential to take the organization to the next level.

Very little escapes the notice of a good leader. That's because good leaders have both eyes wide open.

Leaders value time.

"Everything comes to those
who hustle while they wait."

—Thomas A. Edison

TIME

To say that time is money is an insult to the power of time. Leaders know that time is their most precious commodity, valued even above wealth. They hold the currency of twenty-four precious hours in their hands. The use of these hours will determine success or failure, want or gain. Effective leaders lord over time. They make its minutes and seconds their slaves in order to accomplish their purpose.

They start meetings on time and end the same way. They set sensible borders to house deliberations or planning.

They don't use ten words when one will do. Their presentations are well-planned, relevant, and interesting, but also concise.

They relax, but never dally. They are alert to their prime time—the hours of the day when they are most effective. They pause to regroup physically and mentally.

Effective leaders plan their time well. Each day has an agenda, whether formal or informal. Nothing is done without a purpose, even if that purpose is rest.

A leader considers killing time to be a capital crime.

Leaders prioritize tasks to be done.

"You will never find time for anything. If you want time you must make it!"

—Charles Burton

PRIORITY

Ineffective leaders do the obvious things first. Effective leaders do the *important* things first. A good leader knows that *urgent* and *vital* are not equivalent terms. Many tasks cry out for attention. But the effective leader decides which of those tasks are truly important to the achievement of a goal.

Simple urgency is not enough. The task must be vital to the mission. Every movement must be intricately linked to the core values and purpose of the organization. That demands the leader's focus. In the busyness of the day, the question must be asked: "Does this activity work toward accomplishing our purpose?"

Good leaders understand that not every vital task can be done at once. Some activities will be more important tomorrow than they are today. Careful selection is a mark of leadership. A firm grasp of *when* is just as important as grasping what, who, or how in the management of a project.

Leaders set priorities. They ask, "If I can accomplish only one thing today, what will it be?"

Leaders are credible.

"Trust is the foundation
of leadership."

—Michael Estep

CREDIBILITY

Telling the truth is important; being believed is more important. Having a plan is important; having followers to implement the plan is more important. Good leaders are credible. They're known for getting it right the first time and every time thereafter.

Part of their credibility comes from their vulnerability. Leaders admit their mistakes candidly. They don't try to hide behind the weakness of another. They're willing to say, "Present," when the roll is called. Since they have done their work faithfully, they're not afraid of an inspection by peers. The motives of credible leaders will stand up in a court of public opinion.

They're trustworthy—that is, worthy of trust. They are consistent. They don't hedge the truth or evade the question. And their word and work are as good tomorrow as they were yesterday. Leaders don't shirk either danger or duty. They can be trusted to carry the baton, and they can be trusted to pass it to another when the time comes.

Leaders know that when credibility speaks, the crowd listens.

Leaders put actions to their ideas.

"Fear of ideas makes us impotent and ineffective."

—William O. Douglas

ACTION

In the world of the five-second sound byte, ideas must be able to leap off the page and accomplish something. Leaders who can think may be good analysts, but they will never be effective until they learn to enact their ideas. Action moves theory from the niceties of the page to the needs of the people.

"He talks a good game" is a death knell when applied to a leader. Theories and principles must be tried on the playing field, and leaders are anxious to put them into play. Their actions spring from the wisdom of their maturity.

They act carefully. Effective leaders understand the importance of timing. They act prudently. Their actions are based on their knowledge of available resources. They refuse to commit their team to a cause that has no obvious means of support.

They act courageously. Effective leaders are not afraid to wield the machete in the jungle. They are willing to carve out new paths, to go where no one else has dared to go.

A leader's actions speak louder than words.

Leaders are decision makers.

"Efficiency is doing things right.
Effectiveness is doing
the right thing."

—Alan Nelson

DECISIVENESS

Leaders never flinch when confronted with a choice. It's their job to make decisions, and they're good at it. They know that hesitancy is a dangerous malady that infects and eventually ruins organizations. Sails must be hoisted while the winds blow. Character is built in the now. Leaders are decisive.

They make calculated decisions. Leaders know there are two important paths. One is a road to possible riches, while the other is the road to eventual ruin. Leaders are skilled in choosing the right path. They assess options, weigh priorities, and consult advisors. They make choices. Theirs is an educated determination based on their experience and the wisdom of others.

Leaders make objective decisions. They never hedge a decision based on popular opinion. They're willing to move forward without regard to the personal cost.

Leaders don't procrastinate. When it's time to decide, they pay their money and get on the ride.

Leaders don't put off until tomorrow what they can decide today.

Leaders love people.

"You can give without loving,
but you cannot love
without giving."

—Mark Graham

CARING

It's possible to be a boss without being close to your subordinates. But you can't be a leader without caring about your associates. Why? No one will follow! Leaders do not use people to accomplish a goal. They have genuine concern about their team members.

Lots of people have good ideas. Many people are effective managers. But those who rise to become leaders are those who love people and are loved in return. Associates must know the leader is truly interested in the things that cause them concern. They are not robots that need polishing, but rather human beings who need embracing.

Leaders are not afraid to draw their associates into their circle of acceptance. They respect the correctness of space, but they're willing to cross over the imaginary emotional lines that separate staff and subordinates on the organizational flowchart.

What's the difference between a boss and a leader? The boss has employees. The leader develops leaders. His or her followers know the leader cares about them, their families, and their future.

Leaders are inclusive, not exclusive.

Leaders
always involve others.

"Good leadership is motivating
and mobilizing others to
accomplish a task or to think
in ways that are for the
benefit of all concerned."

—Don Page

INVOLVEMENT

There's a reason why Mrs. Thornapple gives every second grader a part in the Christmas play. She knows that all the parents —and most of the grandparents—will come to watch their child perform. Involvement breeds success. Greater involvement breeds greater success.

The best leaders aren't interested in taking credit, so they don't hoard responsibility. They're interested in reaching the goal, so they involve as many people as they can. They know shared responsibility involves learning and growing experiences for their associates. A constant huddle does not make a championship team. Practice and playing time are where the experience is gained. Perfection is formed on the court or on the field. It doesn't happen in the stands or on the bench.

The robin clears its nest so its young may try their wings. Flight may be terror-filled at first, but the robins' journeys to new horizons begin there. If the mother robin continues to do all the flying and gathering of food, the young will never learn the joy of risk or responsibility.

Real leaders create an open system for involvement.

Leaders think creatively.

"Imagination is the beginning of creativity."

—George Bernard Shaw

CREATIVITY

Leaders don't just think outside the box. They *live* outside the box! If there is a conventional way to approach a problem, a great leader will think of that last. What's new? What's different? What hasn't been done? These are the questions a leader asks.

Leaders are creative people. They see things that don't exist and bring them to life. They are content to work in fresh soil. They don't need the tried and tested. They are willing to go where no one else has gone before. They are moon walkers.

Creative leaders are willing to sacrifice the immediate for the cause of tomorrow. No price is too great to see the birth of their dreams. They're willing to work under the heat of the sun to plant seeds of promise. Clouds and rain don't deter them.

Creative leaders are willing to use methods that haven't been proven. They delight in merging new ideas and principles with people in a fresh coalescence to achieve their goals.

Leaders look at life through the binoculars of possibility.

Leaders are goal-driven.

"We can do anything we want as long as we stick to it."

—Helen Keller

DRIVE

L eaders like to reach the destination. They may enjoy the journey, but they enjoy the arrival even more. Leaders are the people who like to check off every item on the list, and they push to get one more task accomplished at the end of the day.

Leaders have set their sights on a goal, and they clearly understand that reaching *for* that goal is crucial to achieving it. They are driven to push the envelope of effort to get to where they believe they are going.

Leaders have an inner source of refreshment. They have drilled through the sandy soil to the spiritual wellsprings. They keep the pipeline of inspiration open, and they draw freely until their souls are rejuvenated with new strength.

Leaders are guides who point out the mile markers and the objective to their team. They look for creative ways to keep both the purpose and the plan before their associates. And they are restless until the objective has been achieved.

Leaders run until they break the tape.

Leaders are team builders.

"Coming together is a
beginning; keeping
together is progress;
working together is success."

—Henry Ford

TEAMWORK

Marathon runners are rugged athletes. But usually they are not leaders; they compete alone. Leadership is a team sport. It means getting everyone involved in reaching the goal. Leaders do more than direct individuals. They build a team. They gather the separate strengths and abilities of individuals and incorporate them into a working unit. Leaders have both personal goals and corporate goals. They strive to excel individually, but their greatest delight is helping the whole team achieve.

Leaders understand the importance of good communication. They know that the purpose of the team is mere paper until the team members internalize it. They know that without the team members' interaction, the work will be disjointed and the workers will be divided.

Leaders build morale and create community. They keep the mood positive. They compliment and praise individual and team efforts. They celebrate victories and share setbacks. They recognize outstanding achievements because they know that propelling one of the team members forward will push the rest of the team to achieve more.

Leadership is one part leader and nine parts team.

Leaders are unselfish.

"People who live for self
never succeed in satisfying
self or anybody else."

—Trumbull

HUMILITY

A leader who is looking for credit will soon be a solo performer. No team will truly follow a selfish leader. They may establish a work regimen, but they will work without real respect. The best leaders display that seldom-seen virtue—humility. They discover real worth in terms of their ability to generate team excellence.

They don't care who gets the praise, as long as the job gets done. Actions take precedence over accolades. Goals are more important than gold. Ribbons are incidental to right behavior. Great leaders don't draw attention to themselves. They express their appreciation for the contributions of others.

They're willing to put the mission ahead of their own desires. They've discovered the greater joy of giving their lives for something worthwhile. The purpose, mission, and objectives of the organization are paramount, while the personalities and personal achievements of the leader are secondary. What they have done as individuals is far less important than what they have done to help others succeed.

The bigger the leader, the smaller the ego!

Leaders ask directions.

"A word spoken in due
season, how good it is!"

—Proverbs 15:23 NKJV

ADVICE

Good leaders don't try to be experts in every area. Leaders know what they *don't* know. They understand the limitations of their wisdom and experience, but they are willing to fill in the gaps by asking directions from others. They know that they have skills, but they also know that they are within a question's reach of even broader skills. They understand that the winds of changing technologies will blow them away unless they find a fresh resource for learning.

People who don't ask for counsel make unnecessary mistakes. Leaders are not bashful about asking advice. They cultivate counselors. They work on developing a network of associates who will be able to plug modules of skill and experience into their lives.

They begin their search for advice at home. They are sensitive to the abilities and experience of their own associates. They seek input from the team and ask questions. They know that there's no shame in being ignorant, but it's a crime to be negligent.

The wisest leaders are those with the wisest advisors.

Leaders believe in win-win.

"You can get everything you want if you help enough others get what they want."

—Zig Ziglar

MUTUALITY

Success is not a zero-sum enterprise. Good leaders know that their achievement doesn't require someone else's failure. There's more than enough success to go around. The most effective leaders are those who believe their success can help others reach their goals also. They believe in the power of win-win.

Leaders ask, "What can I do for you?" They understand that by helping others, they are benefiting themselves. Service is an investment that pays in more than monetary ways. It pays in character development. It pays in influence and in relationships. Giving is a short-term investment that pays long-term dividends.

Leaders ask, "What can we do together?" Teamwork is a win-win situation. Working as a team, leaders gain from the abilities of others. First, they gain the knowledge of those abilities. Working with others teaches them how the task is accomplished. Second, they gain the effect of those abilities. They share the acclaim brought to the team by the effectiveness of its members. It's a win-win situation.

Leaders ask, "How can this benefit both of us?"

Leaders get acquainted with the team.

"To be rich in friends is to be poor in nothing."

—Lilian Whiting

RELATIONSHIP

It's impossible to lead from arm's length. Good leaders rub shoulders with the team. They know that they don't necessarily have to become "one of the gang," but they take the time to get acquainted with their associates.

Leaders find ways to create a relationship with the team. They remember names, join in conversations, and take part in the team's social events. They are as willing to share a laugh as they are to share a tear, rejoicing with those who rejoice and grieving with those who grieve. They acknowledge a team member's setback with sympathy and acknowledge a team member's accomplishment with praise.

Leaders aren't afraid to roll their sleeves up. They know that some of their most valued relationships will be won in the trenches. Their associates learn by their mutual teamwork that no one is above the goals and purpose of the organization. They learn that the job will get done only when the team works together in unity.

Leaders know the importance of getting to know their team.

Leaders
accept good feedback.

"Success in any area requires
constantly readjusting your
behavior as a result
of feedback."

—Michael Gelb

OPENNESS

The person who tells you that your slip is showing before you stand up to address an audience is not your enemy. That person is your friend. Leaders understand the difference between helpful feedback and spiteful criticism. They welcome the former and ignore the latter.

In one sense, leaders are pollsters. Their success depends on the favor of the people. Consequently, they want to know how the tides of opinion are flowing. They are always seeking ways to have an impact upon their "market." For example, when the report doesn't communicate clearly, they want to know why. The helpful suggestions of their associates are the building blocks of success, not stumbling blocks of negativism.

Leaders value "field reports." They don't want to spin the wheels of a principle or technology that does not move the organization forward. Constructive criticism doesn't roll off their backs like water off a duck. They gather and sort it to see if it has the potential to grow into excellence.

Leaders are more interested in fixing problems than in passing blame.

Leaders provide resources to do the job.

"A good objective of leadership is to help those who are doing poorly to do well and to help those who are doing well to do even better."

—Jim Rohn

ENABLING

Rocket ships are not built by superheroes. They're built by ordinary people who have been given the right training, skills, and equipment to do the job. Leaders are the ones who bring the people and resources together.

A sales force needs a product. The leader makes sure it's in supply by developing the concept or the sales item, assembling the marketing plan, and equipping the salesperson with training in presentation and sales techniques.

A programmer needs data. The leader keeps the flow of information heading in the programmer's direction. A leader understands that part of his or her responsibility is breaking bottlenecks. By quick attention to the lack of flow, the leader helps to eliminate job stress and misunderstanding among the associates.

Leaders enable others to work by providing resources. They unleash the creative power of their team by providing the right tools. They make continuing education a priority by encouraging their associates to develop their skills in both on-site and off-site training opportunities.

Leaders keep the well of available resources flowing freely.

Leaders clearly define job duties.

"People perform better when leadership roles are defined."

—Stan Toler

EXPECTATIONS

A good team will do whatever it's asked to do. But the team members must know what it is they're being asked to do! It's the leader's job to define expectations. Many team members are ineffective and unproductive simply because they have no clear focus. They're willing, and they're able. They just don't understand what is expected of them.

A good leader lets every team member know exactly what his or her responsibilities are. First, a leader clearly communicates the purpose for the assignment. Second, he or she clearly outlines a job description. Associates must understand their roles in helping the organization reach its goals. Areas of responsibility are spelled out to avoid overlap and misunderstanding among team members.

Productivity depends on accountability, and accountability begins with expectations. Good leaders give the team an opportunity to report back. They know that if an assignment is open-ended, it may never be completed. Leaders form the borders of responsibility, and they serve as a "border patrol" to make sure the project is accomplished within the confines of the border.

The leader's expectations never exceed their explanations.

Leaders
celebrate milestones.

"Talent does you no good
unless it is recognized
by someone else."

—Robert Half

RECOGNITION

Leaders celebrate the giant steps taken by their team. They recognize the milestones along the journey. When the newest team member completes training, the whistles blow. When the first quarter objectives are met, the balloons go up. When the goal is reached, it's lunch on the house. Good leaders take every opportunity to reinforce the team's progress.

Leaders understand the importance of recognition. They know that one who feels appreciated for his or her effort accomplishes a job well done. Leaders don't wait for the retirement party to hand out the roses. They do it on a regular basis. Those blips on the team member's résumé do not go unnoticed. Every step up the ladder is noteworthy (and worthy of a note).

Leaders are constantly waving the banner that says, "Way to go! We're on the right track!" They know that the verbal, written, or tangible expressions of their approval propel the team forward. Morale soars as every member comes to see that his or her victory is helping to pull the train.

Leaders are cheerleaders.

Leaders recognize team excellence.

"The best leader brings out the best in those he has stewardship over."

—J. Richard Clarke

PRAISE

Top performers don't work just for money. They're also motivated by an internal desire to achieve. Workers who are concerned with excellence have an inner source of inspiration. They are driven to do their best by an ethic obviously so rare that few seek to adopt it. Good leaders know when they have found those excellence seekers, and they tap their hidden resources by praising their achievements.

Leaders know which team members are the standouts. Peak performers are usually the first in line and the last to leave. They are usually those who are the last to complain and the first to cooperate. They are not inconvenienced by an assignment, because they have already sacrificed convenience for the greater cause.

Leaders understand the value of half-time speeches. But they know that constructive criticism is best mixed with constructive encouragement. They understand the leadership theory that performance expands in proportion to the praise that has been poured in. When the team goes the extra mile, the leader goes overboard to recognize the sacrifice.

Leaders have an eye for excellence.

Leaders focus on the mission.

"A good leader remains focused.
Controlling your destination
is better than being
controlled by it."

—Jack Welch

FOCUS

Distractions are the bane of the ineffective leader. Like a hound chasing two rabbits at once, the unproductive leader changes directions frequently. Consequently, his or her followers become confused and frustrated. Never knowing exactly what to do, they usually end up doing nothing.

But productive leaders have a single focus. They "chase" one thing at a time. They've narrowed their attention. They know what needs to done, and they know what they will have to do to accomplish it. They've zeroed in on the mission.

They also know what resources are available to carry out the mission. They know how to gather manpower for the task. Focused leaders usually don't lack followers. People with a mind to work naturally gravitate to someone who is able to give them good directions.

Effective leaders understand what team skills are needed. They know who the team specialists are, and they understand whose individual talents are best suited for the assignment.

Effective leaders are not interested in doing ten good things. They want to do one thing and do it right.

Leaders understand role definition.

"Learning is a treasure that accompanies its owner everywhere."

—Chinese Proverb

ROLE

Stand a punter next to an offensive tackle, and you'll understand why football players have clearly defined positions. Five or six inches and a hundred pounds will tell you that these people have different responsibilities on the football field. Not only do leaders understand their own function—their role—they also know the roles of the other members on their team.

Part of the leader's task is to help each team member understand his or her place on the team. Good leaders have given this old adage a new meaning: A place for everyone and everyone in his place. Just as the master chess player knows how each chess piece functions in its position on the chessboard, leaders know how to match the person with the position. They understand the position. They don't assign team members to a responsibility that isn't clearly understood.

Then they train the team. Good leaders never ask people to function in ways they're not equipped to serve.

Leaders know how to place people in their best positions.

Leaders are willing to ask forgiveness.

"The price of greatness
is responsibility."

—Winston Churchill

RESPONSIBILITY

Good leaders act responsibly. They don't need to be told when they're wrong. More often than not, they'll tell you. They manifest in their own lives the personal openness and honesty they expect from their associates.

Leaders can't afford to be defensive about personal failure. Too many other things are at stake to worry about saving face. The team member who spends an inordinate amount of time reflecting on the last play is one who probably won't have the courage to execute the next one.

Leaders are willing to take responsibility for their actions. They're willing to go down the checklist of their own attitudes and motivations to see if they are the sand particle in the machinery that keeps it from running smoothly. They are willing to make the personal sacrifice for the overall welfare of the organization.

"I was wrong." "I am sorry." The sentences are rather small, but they are highly significant. And they will make a far greater impact than a long speech about morale and team effort.

Leaders are peacemakers.

Leaders multiply their effectiveness by training potential leaders.

"There is nothing training cannot do. Nothing is above its reach."

—Mark Twain

MULTIPLICATION

Leaders expand their work by multiplication, not just by addition. An experienced leader is always on the lookout for a talented newcomer. Leaders know they are limited by time and space to meet all the needs of the organization. Adding an additional worker may not be enough, however. New teams will have to be formed. New workers will have to be recruited. One of the first lessons of leadership is that one person cannot do everything. But everything that needs to be accomplished *can* be accomplished through the recruitment, training, and empowering of others.

Every leader's goal should be to train his or her replacement. The organization's effectiveness depends on multiplying its leadership. It's simple arithmetic. "You take over here, and I'll start a new team over there." What's the result? "Yesterday there were ten of us. Tomorrow there'll be twenty." How will that affect the organization? "Yesterday we could only do *this much*, because there were so few of us. Today and tomorrow we can do *that much*, because there are more of us."

Leaders spend time recruiting leaders.

Leaders select team members who work well with others.

"The achievements of an organization are the results of the combined efforts of each individual."

—Vince Lombardi

COMPATIBILITY

The saying, "You can't mix oil and water," is a painful reminder. Often that expression comes from the battlefields of interpersonal relationships. Coworkers have disagreed over policies or methods. They shared an assignment, but they are not kindred spirits. A leader has to make important choices when building a team. Some people work well with others. Some don't. The leader's job is to find the right combinations of personality, skill, and zeal.

Some very gifted people don't work well with others. They are solo performers. They'll achieve more on their own than if they were burdened with two assistants.

Others work like oxen. They're best when paired. They like the camaraderie of the work environment. They feed off the companionship of others. They work better when they're teamed with one or more team members.

Wise leaders recognize these traits and build the team accordingly. They don't try to make a "people person" out of a "lone wolf." They yoke performers with people who possess complementary strengths in order to accomplish their purpose.

Good leaders are matchmakers.

Leaders seek to understand chemistry.

"Leaders always find a way
to make things happen."

—John Maxwell

CHEMISTRY

Whether cultivated or innate, leaders have an understanding of the psychology of the team. They observe group dynamics. They understand the "group think" of their teams. They know what motivates people to excellence, and they know what impedes their progress.

The leader knows when the team members need encouragement and when they need rest. He or she is alert to the signs of fatigue and stress. The leader knows when a "pause" will put the team on "fast forward." He or she also understands the power of a good *word* in propelling the team to good *work*.

The leader also knows when to encourage and when to rebuke. Knowing the team members' strengths and weaknesses, the leader knows when they are performing at their best or working beneath it. The skillful acknowledgment of that effort, or lack of effort, can be a great motivator.

Call it dime-store psychology, the best leaders know what makes the team tick—and they use that knowledge to move the members toward the goal.

Leaders know when to push and when to pull.

Leaders value team diversity.

"Two are better than one, because they have a good return on their work: If one falls down, his friend can help him up. But pity the man who falls and has no one to help him up!"

—Ecclesiastes 4:9-10

UNIQUENESS

People are like snowflakes. There are no two alike. A good leader understands that concept and treats team members as individuals. Vibrant leadership avoids "cookie cutter" management. Some people just won't be put into a mold. They inwardly rebel at best and revolt openly at worst.

The very thing that would excite one worker to excellence might cause another worker to question his or her ability. You might take a direct approach with one associate, pointing out weak areas that need to be strengthened. The same direct-criticism approach with another team member may result in discouragement and distrust. A good leader won't offer Bob the same encouragement that motivates John. A good leader won't ask Jane to work for the same reward as Jill.

Leaders understand that people are different and make it a point to understand that uniqueness in their team members. Some would call that a good management technique. Good leaders think of it as common courtesy. They treat others as they themselves would like to be treated.

Leaders know that one size doesn't fit all.

Leaders know how to evaluate their efforts.

"What happens to a man is less significant than what happens within him."

—Louis L. Mann

SELF-EVALUATION

Neither congratulations nor criticism should take a leader by surprise. That's because no friend or detractor can say anything that the leader doesn't already know. Leaders who examine themselves will avoid being swayed by flattery or wounded by criticism. They know their strengths and weaknesses. They know when they are in a success mode, and they know when they're heading in the wrong direction.

They can accept praise without becoming conceited. They know that many of their accomplishments come from the contributions of their associates. When they accept the applause of others, they are inwardly extending a hand toward their team members.

And they can listen to criticism without taking offense. Since they have a great sense of purpose and direction, constructive criticism can only help to propel them toward their objectives.

Good leaders are comfortable in their own skin. They know what's true about them, and they don't mind hearing it. They also know their weakness, and so they listen to the suggestions that will help them fulfill their leadership role.

Leaders are honest with themselves.

Leaders celebrate the special days of team members.

"Unless we think of others
and do something for them,
we miss one of the greatest
sources of happiness."

—Ray Lyman Wilbur

COMMUNITY

Birthdays, anniversaries, graduations, births—these events mark the passage of life. Good leaders are aware of the life stages of their team members. By celebrating these special days, they affirm their team members' value.

It's not difficult. The office get-well card, for example, is not an administrative chore. It's a tangible way to say, "I care about this incident in your life because I care about you." The office birthday party is not an excuse to stop work. It's a team-building activity. It's a morale booster. By recognizing the milestone, the leader is showing the honoree and the attendees that they are important on a personal level, not just at an organizational level.

Births, deaths, weddings—because these events in the lives of the organization's team are so important, effective leaders make them a priority. If a personal visit is possible, it is far preferred over a "Hallmark moment." Every opportunity to celebrate an accomplishment or life transition communicates concern to the team.

Leaders are always alert to the "precious moments" of their associates.

Leaders blame quietly.

"Leaders praise loudly
and blame softly."

—Catherine the Great (adapted)

TACT

From time to time, the best interest of the organization is served by a leader's reprimand of an associate. How that task is handled is a mark of effective leadership. There's an old proverb that says, "Do not use a hatchet to remove a fly from your friend's forehead."

Effective leaders are tactful. While praise is given in the hearing of others, rebuke is made in private. They never berate or belittle their associates. Their critique is always wrapped in a blanket of kindness. Seldom will the harsh treatment of a team member result in better performance. Bitterness, not "betterness," is usually the result.

Also, leaders know that the critique is more effective when it is "sandwiched" between compliments. Recognizing the good qualities of an associate makes the reminder of a problem area much easier to digest.

Always, the critique is made for redemptive purposes. It is to raise the performance level of the team member—to point out the weakness in order to turn it into a strength.

A good leader protects the self-esteem of the team.

Leaders listen and respond.

"Whoever gives heed to instruction prospers, and blessed is he who trusts in the Lord."

—Proverbs 16:20

RESPONSIVENESS

All leaders listen—sooner or later. Good leaders listen early. They are responsive to honest feedback and good suggestions.

Leaders listen to their "customers." Whether in business or ministry, they know that they have a product to sell to the public. What does the customer want? Effective leaders not only listen, they respond by going the extra mile in trying to meet customer needs.

Leaders listen to their team. What do the team members need? What are their suggestions for greater organizational efficiency? How are they relating to the leadership? To each other? By carefully listening and responding, the leader can make quick improvements that will dramatically affect the organization.

Leaders listen to other leaders. Like a golfer learning from the previous putt on the green, a leader "goes to school" on the experience of others.

Leaders listen to their own instincts. They understand that "gut feelings" are often dependable barometers. They learn to respond to their inner voice and take positions that sometimes even go against the grain of the organization.

Leaders have ears to hear.

Leaders are self-controlled.

"Champions don't become
champions in the field—they
are merely recognized there."

—Bob Costas

DISCIPLINE

Effective leaders know how to discipline themselves in order to reach their goals. Ineffective leaders place their personal comfort or interests above the mission. Their efforts are sporadic, and, subsequently, their record of achievement is checkered.

Effective leaders have disciplined work habits. They are dependable, punctual, consistent, and trustworthy. Leaders know how to focus on a project, avoid distractions, and move toward a stated goal.

Effective leaders have disciplined personal habits. They know that sobriety, moderation, and an even temper are character qualities that will benefit them throughout their lives; so they work at these qualities. They take care of their bodies. They exercise. They eat wisely. They get plenty of rest.

Effective leaders have disciplined spiritual habits. They spend time in reverent reflection and worship. They read inspirational books and listen to inspiring tapes. They read the Bible. They spend time communing with God in prayer.

Discipline is not optional. Leaders know that a steady, sustained effort is necessary to accomplish the mission.

Leaders put themselves on a short leash.

Leaders really care about people.

"People don't care how much
you know until they know
how much you care."

—Howard Hendricks

CARING

Leaders take a genuine interest in their followers. For a good leader, building up the team is high on the agenda. Next to spiritual commitments, a commitment to others is a primary leadership quality. Wisdom and skill are necessary, but without an ability to relate to others in a caring way, the leader's impact will be insignificant. Leaders care about the concerns of others.

They care about the personal welfare of their associates and relate to them on a personal level. They not only know their names, they know their likes and dislikes. They know their hobbies. They know where they came from and where they're going; they know their background; and they know as much about their future plans as they possibly can.

They realize that each of their associates has an extended family. And that extended family has achievements or setbacks that will directly affect the attitude of the associate. By expressing an interest in the extended family, the leader expresses a personal concern that ties him or her to the team member.

Leaders like people.

Leaders acknowledge their weaknesses.

"An honest man is the noblest work of God."

—Alexander Pope

TRANSPARENCY

Good leaders are not afraid to admit weakness. In fact, they honestly examine themselves in order to identify areas of need. In being transparent about themselves, they can focus on turning their weaknesses into strengths.

Effective leaders don't have to be right all the time. They're not control freaks. They're humble enough to acknowledge their achievements and to admit when they've been a part of the problem rather than the solution.

Effective leaders are willing to acknowledge the things they don't know. In today's highly evolving society, precepts and methods change almost daily. Leaders try to swim in the currents of that ever-changing technology.

Also, effective leaders are willing to acknowledge the things they can't do. They don't *fear* incompetence; they just *fight* it. They are constantly developing their skills and creating new solutions to old problems.

Effective leaders aren't afraid to ask for help. By doing so, they not only open the door to self-improvement, but they also gain personal strength.

Leaders live in the construction zone.

Leaders are servants.

"Be ashamed to die until
you have done something
for humanity."

—General Douglas MacArthur

SERVICE

Many people see the leader as the person on top—the one with the perks, the privileges, and the praise. That's a myth. The truth is, leaders are at the bottom of the pyramid. It's the leader who bears responsibility for the group, not vice versa. It's the leader who must form the chain of productivity by using the very human links of associates and team members. The pressure of service is on the leader.

It's the leader who must make the hard decisions deciding quickly and carefully who goes and who remains, or making the painful decisions that plug the money flow. It's the leader who must ensure that the needs of the group are met and who is responsible for making the work or ministry environment either happy or horrible. The leader must go the extra mile if the organization is going to go farther down the road.

The leader is a servant of all, not the greatest of all.

Leaders take time for their families.

"It is a wise father who knows his child. But maybe it's a very wise child who takes time to know his father."

—Anonymous

FAMILY

Good leaders don't build an empire on the backs of their children. They recognize that their responsibility to family must come before their commitments to a vocation, or even their desire to succeed. Leaders understand that the happiness of their homes directly influences the happiness of their work. So they make the time and the effort to contribute to that happiness.

Leaders take time to communicate with their spouses. They don't leave their listening ears at the office. They share their dreams, update their spouses on their organizational plans, and seek their spouses' advice. They treat their spouses better than their most trusted associates.

Leaders are available for their children. They know when to leave the office and head for the ballpark. They know how to push the pause button on their plans and productivity. Leaders give more than passing attention to birthdays and report cards. They don't send representatives to the school play.

Leaders make sure that, of all the people who compete for their attention, their families get first priority.

Leaders guard home base.

Leaders stay current.

"As a rule, he or she who has
the most information will have
the greatest success in life."

—Disraeli

KNOWLEDGE

There was a farmer who posted this sign on the pasture fence: "Trespassers are welcome. Just be sure to cross the field in 9.9 seconds. The bull can make it in ten!" In this fast-moving age of information, it's easy to get left behind. Leaders try to stay ahead of charging bulls by staying alert and by staying informed.

They read constantly. They learn how to pick the meat off an article or a news item and leave the bones. They know what's in the news, and they keep up on trade journals. There's always a book on their nightstand.

They learn while they're on the move. They beg, borrow, or buy tapes of specialists in their area and play them when they're mobile.

They attend seminars and workshops and take every opportunity to learn from the best in their field. They take notes, file their notes, and then utilize them.

Leaders thirst for understanding and insight. But they understand that knowledge is not a pond; it's a river.

Leaders wade out into the current.

Leaders are organized.

"Either you run the day or
the day runs you."

—J. C. McPheeters

ORGANIZATION

A worker is responsible for one thing. Leaders are responsible for many things. They are skilled in managing a myriad of details. The most successful leaders are those who are best organized.

Day planners, pert charts, and Palm Pilots are not gimmicks or gadgets. They are the tools of a successful leader. They are as vital to him or her as the carpenter's hammer, the electrician's pliers, or the piano tuner's tuning fork. Effective leaders use them to track projects, manage assignments, and keep their appointments.

A good leader will not know the answer to every question. But this is certain: he or she will know where to find it. Discoveries once made only by searching through expensive desk-reference sets are now only a mouse click away. The Internet's virtual library is never closed.

Organization is not only necessary for multitasking, it's a defining quality for successful leadership. Modern managers must be skilled in knowing where things are, keeping them in order, and being able to retrieve them at a moment's notice.

Leaders are finders and keepers.

Leaders make team meetings work.

"Everything is created twice—
first mentally, then physically."

—Greg Anderson

CONTROL

Just as a sports team needs a huddle to talk about its plays and assignments, organizations need meetings to map strategies and discuss responsibilities. Depending on their leadership, those meetings are either enjoyed by the team or they are endured.

Nobody likes an aimless meeting. So a good leader must walk the fine line between liberty and authority to make team meetings work.

There are some common characteristics of a good team meeting however. A good team meeting has a clear agenda. Effective leaders determine the priorities for the meeting and post them in a carefully arranged order.

A good team meeting starts and ends on time. Effective leaders do their best to start the meeting at the announced time, and they tactfully bring the discussion to an end when the announced closing time approaches.

A good team meeting has a focused discussion. A poor leader stifles discussion. A poorer leader allows the dialogue to become chatter. The best leader has a destination for every meeting and helps the team arrive there on time.

Leaders are conductors.

Leaders catch people doing something right.

"Practice random acts
of kindness and senseless
acts of beauty."

—Adair Lara

REINFORCEMENT

Good leaders know that more flies are caught with honey than with vinegar. People respond best to positive reinforcement. So leaders are quick to notice the good in the attitudes and actions of their associates. And they not only notice it, they mention it. Encouragement is one of the key qualities of effective leadership. Leaders are encouragers.

They set clear goals for each team member and offer lots of support along the way. They always have an encouraging word for the dedicated efforts of their team. They don't ignore random acts of dedication.

When a worker's performance improves, they point it out. When a team member meets an objective, they offer on-the-spot congratulations. Leaders don't assume that everyone knows of team improvements. They make it a practice to mention the team's forward motion. They let people know what they are doing right—specifically. "You're doing a great job!" has greater meaning when specifics are added: "You're doing a great job in leading that small-group discussion!" The specifics are the icing on the celebration cake.

Leaders are *good*-watchers.

Leaders work smarter.

"God gives us the ingredients
for our daily bread, but He
expects us to do the baking."

—William Arthur Ward

DISCERNMENT

Working twice as hard is hardly ever the solution to a problem. It usually gets you nowhere twice as fast. Leaders look for ways to improve the process, rather than simply increasing the effort. They understand the negative impact of fatigue on their bodies, minds, and spirits. So they discern ways to beat the demons—ways to work smarter, not harder. They ask the two most important questions in any enterprise: *"Why?"* and *"What if?"*

"Why is our output down, even when our manpower is up?" Leaders look for underlying causes, getting to the very core of the production problem. "What are the hindrances?" "Who are the bottleneckers?"

"Why do we need this step in our process?" Leaders look for organizational overlap. They sort out methods that are based merely on tradition. They look for shortcuts that won't shortchange the organization.

Leaders also ask the important "What if?" questions. "What if we shifted that responsibility to someone else?" "What if we eliminated this task?" They have a discerning eye for what works best.

Leaders are thinkers.

Leaders empower and release the team.

"The best executive is the one
who has sense enough to pick
good men to do what he wants
done, and self-restraint enough
to keep from meddling
while they do it."

—Teddy Roosevelt

EMPOWERMENT

The greatest barrier to effective leadership is the desire to control others. Tight control breeds low morale and ineffective performance among team members. Micromanagement stifles the creativity and natural ability that teammates bring to a project.

Good leaders know that more is accomplished by *empowering* others than by *commanding* them. By duplicating their knowledge and skills in the life of an associate, leaders get twice as much accomplished. But knowledge without opportunity is useless. Associates must have a free hand to experiment with their new insight and understanding.

Leaders seek to release the team, not imprison it. They look for ways the team members can "try their wings." They create opportunities for team members to assume leadership roles. They divide the workload, create new teams, and assign tasks. Leaders are constantly empowering their associates to fulfill the mission of the organization.

Motivation, encouragement, inspiration, support—these are the weapons of the greatest generals. They don't rigidly manage their troops. Instead, they motivate them to achieve the mission.

Leaders give power to the people.

Leaders understand "roll up your sleeves" commitment.

"When building a team, I always search first for people who love to win. If I can't find any of those, I look for people who hate to lose."

—H. Ross Perot

HARD WORK

Leaders can't pass the buck. It's up to them to get the job done, and they know it. But getting the job done often includes personal sacrifice. Leaders understand that sacrifice begins at the top. When the team works late, they stick with them. When the project bogs down, they pitch in to help.

Leaders understand that meeting objectives means moving beyond paper and planning. There is a need for the huddle. But the progress down the field happens only after the team breaks huddle. That progress is dependent upon team cooperation—cooperation between the leader and the team, and cooperation between team members.

A spirit of cooperation is birthed in the trenches, where leaders show they are not afraid to contribute their own blood, sweat, and tears to the effort.

Working shoulder-to-shoulder with the team, the leader demonstrates commitment to the goal. Morale rises. Productivity improves. Objectives are met. All of this happens when leaders "roll up their sleeves" and stay until the job is done.

Leaders don't just lead the team; they are part of the team.

Leaders
reward excellence.

"Excellence is doing ordinary
things extraordinarily well."

—John W. Gardner

INCENTIVE

Good leaders know which side their bread is buttered on. They understand that the performance of the team is what ensures their own success. So they look for excellence and reward it. Leaders understand that incentives not only help to build morale, they also increase production.

Incentives are offered on an emotional level. Good leaders treat every team member as a volunteer. Knowing that high achievers could choose to work anywhere, they give those stars a reason to stay where they are. They make sure they are appreciated. They praise their good performance. They are friendly and supportive. They call them by name and treat them as personal friends.

Incentives are also offered on a tangible level. They offer bonuses when possible and award trophies or plaques for high achievement. They celebrate milestones of service with a dinner. They reward faithful service with a write-up in the trade journals. They assign reserved parking places. Leaders are always looking for the team member who goes the extra mile.

Leaders are stargazers.

Leaders soar like eagles.

"The most effective way to achieve right relationships is to look for the best in every person, and then help that best into its fullest expression."

—Allen J. Boone

ACHIEVEMENT

A leader, by definition, is out in front of others. The leader is the person who rises above the crowd, pointing the way to worthwhile goals. It's the leader who dreams big dreams and makes them come true. It's the leader who points to the mountaintop and takes others there.

Leaders are achievers who soar to new heights, who accomplish great things. They are not afraid to go where no one else has gone. They're willing to abandon the nest, to catch the current no matter where it may take them, to risk everything for a higher purpose. The wind in their face doesn't hamper them; rather it causes them to climb even higher.

It's the leader who has the faith to envision the world as being different than it is and the fortitude to make it so. Leaders are not content with mediocrity. Through eyes of faith, they see a world free from the problems they believe they can solve, and their vision is contagious.

Leaders aren't afraid to take the leap.

Leaders march to the mission.

"The growth and development
of people is the highest
calling of leadership."

—Harvey S. Firestone

SINGLE-MINDEDNESS

Good leaders have little trouble organizing the tasks for any given day. "What matters most?" is the question they ask. "What will contribute to the mission?" they want to know. Everything else is secondary. A good leader is single-minded in pursuit of the goal. He or she will not be distracted by activities that are not mission-focused. Ineffective leaders are drawn by lesser concerns. They entangle themselves in the mundane at the expense of the more important. Consequently, as they chase after unimportant details, they sound an uncertain note to their team members.

Good leaders know what counts, and they do it. Their energies are focused on the things that matter, those that are central to the mission of their organization. Their daily calendars reflect their commitment to the core purpose. Lesser chores are either delegated or dropped.

In one sense, they have tied themselves to a mission. Their goals and objectives reflect it; their peers identify them with it; and nothing can pull them from it.

Leaders have a one-track heart.

Leaders identify core values.

"Try not to become a person
of success but rather a
person of value."

—Albert Einstein

PRINCIPLES

There's a reason why some organizations are marked by honesty and integrity while others aren't. In either case, it's because the leader has set the tone and identified the core values for the team.

"Honesty matters more than success." "We keep our word." "We believe in serving others." Those are the principles of a good organization, principles that have been set by a leader who has modeled them in his or her life. Leaders cannot expect their organization to exemplify principles that they don't espouse themselves. And neither should they expect it from their associates.

"Winning is the only thing that matters." "Do whatever it takes to reach the goal." Those are the principles of a poor organization, and they probably reflect the values of its leader. Poor character qualities have a way of entering the organization through its leadership.

Every organization has core values. Some are negative and unproductive. Others are positive and productive. The leader decides what they will be. Leaders create the culture and ethic for the organization, and subsequently for the entire team.

Leaders care about character.

Leaders seek the guidance of God.

"A leader never lets
adversity get him down—
except on his knees."

—Jim Williams

PRAYER

Everyone depends on the leader for answers. "Where do we go next?" "What's our goal?" "Should we move ahead or wait?" It's the leader who must make the decisions, sometimes choosing between the greater of two goods or the lesser of two evils. Effective leaders have learned this secret of leadership: they are not alone. When forced to make tough choices, they seek the counsel of the One greater than themselves. They seek the guidance of God.

Competence, skill, and intelligence—all of these are important attributes for leadership. But there is one greater: faith. Truly great leaders *believe* in Someone greater than themselves, and they express that belief in regular times of reflection and devotion.

Their times of prayer signify a spiritual relationship with the Almighty that makes them feel accepted and loved, even when their associates or peers have abandoned them.

To them, prayer is not a way out. It is a way through. The strength that is derived from communication with God sustains them through times of adversity.

Leaders have a spiritual support system.